PYTHON PROGRAMMING

Python Programming for Complete Novices

SCOTT BERNARD

Table of Contents

INTRODUCTION

Congratulations on purchasing *Python: Python Programming for Beginners,* and thank you for doing so.

The following chapters will discuss what you are able to learn when using the Python programming language. This is one of the best programming languages, especially for beginners. It is based on the English language and is designed to be easy to read, thanks to the way the program is set up. Python has all the power that you would for your coding language, and it can be combined with other languages, allowing you to accomplish many tasks when writing your code.

This guidebook is going to take time to discuss how to get started with Python. We will start with uploading the program onto your computer, how to write out some of the basic commands of this language, and follow up with which environment you should use to make this happen. Once you have mastered some of the basics, you will be able to move on to working with the decision control structure of the language, how to work with classes and objects, and working with functions. You will be ready to go with your own codes in no time.

Whether you are looking to learn a new coding language or would like to learn your first coding language, Python is one of the best options to explore. Take a look through this guidebook, and take your first steps to becoming familia with the Python programming language.

There are plenty of books on this subject on the market, thanks again for choosing this one! Every effort was made to ensure it is full of as much useful information as possible. Please enjoy!

CHAPTER 1

Understanding The Basics Of Python

There is much one can learn in the world of coding. There are many different coding languages to discover, each with their optimal uses, strengths, and weaknesses. Each coding language has its own way of speaking to the computer to issue commands. Sometimes as a beginner, it is confusing to understand how coding languages work. Perhaps at some point, you have seen complicated code and felt that it was too difficult to grasp. Maybe you listened to others talk about code at some point, and it just seemed to go over your head. While there are some technical aspects to be found in any coding language, all code works to tell the computer how to behave at heart. Once you learn some of the basics, it doesn't have to be difficult.

If you are interested in becoming proficient in coding, Python is a very good starting point. It is a relatively easy language to understand. It is based on English (so there aren't any complicated words to learn along the way). Even if you have no experience with coding, you will find that reading through this language can be simple.

Some other coding languages may have more options or more power compared to Python. C++ is a popular coding language that can be used in hacking, while languages like Java and JavaScript are perfect for setting up web pages online. However, for a complete novice getting started in coding – to build up some of your confidence in how this process works— Python is one of the best that you will find.

When working in Python, you will be able to notice its philosophy fairly early on. This programming language was built on the idea of being simple to use. As a beginner, you will appreciate being able to look at the code and understand what is there, rather than just taking my word for what you write. Most beginners appreciate the simplicity of design of this language.

Some of the benefits and features that you will enjoy when working on Python include:

- The syntax is elegant and easy to read.

- The language is user friendly. Not only will you be able to read through it, but you can also avoid a lot of the bugs and problems that come with the other coding languages.
- The Python library is large. A library is a list of commands that a language can perform, along with a set of instructions on how to use those commands. You will be able to look to it for guidance for some of the tasks that you want to complete when writing your programs. The library is going to include commands that help with connecting to web servers, changing files, searching for text, and more. As a beginner, you should spend some time looking through this library, because it can provide you with valuable points of reference you will need to begin writing code.
- The Python interface is one of the most intuitive. This can make it easy for a beginner to test out their code to see what is working for them. If you want to experiment a bit and see if one technique is better than another, the Python language makes that easier.
- At times, you may want to expand the work that you are doing into something more complex or powerful. Python works great with certain other coding modules, including C++ and C, so you will have this option down the road if you so choose.

- Python is set up to work with all of the operating systems including Mac, Windows, Unix, and Linux.
- The Python program is free. Python is an open source program. This means that its creators wrote the code for it, and released it on the internet (FOR FREE!) to allow other programmers to modify it. You can download it for free and keep it unchanged for your own personal use, or you can choose to edit it and develop a new update, when you gain enough skill and are feeling brave. You can always re-download the original version and start over.
- There are some advanced features that come with this programming language. You will enjoy some of these features, such as generators and comprehensions as you get more advanced in your coding knowledge.
- There is the option to group together codes into modules and packages whenever you need.
- There are many data types that are allowed inside of the Python program. You can pick from the data types of numbers, lists, strings, and dictionaries.
- And finally, it is easy to find errors that occur in the Python language. Since the different data types are going to be dynamic types, when these types come together and get mixed, it is going to raise up an exception that you will need to deal

with inside of your code. More on data types later.

Setting up your computer for Python

There are a few parts that you are going to need to place to make Python work. First, you need to make sure that you have some kind of text editor in place. This is the area where you will write out the codes that you want to work with inside of the Python language. It doesn't have to be anything complicated. When you are working on a Windows computer, you could use the Notepad feature to be your text editor. Other text edit options include Notepad++, WordPad, and Microsoft Word.

Once you have chosen the text editor that you would like to use, it is time to download your Python package. Since this is free, you will be able to pick the version that you like the most, and then get it downloaded in no time. You can visit www.python.org to get a list of the versions that are available, and there you will be able to pick out the one that you would like to use. While you are downloading this, make sure to download the IDLE (Integrated Development and Learning Environment) along with it. Your program is not going to work without this environment being in place. Once you've done all this, it is time to working in Python and start making your own codes.

Reasons to Use Python

As we mentioned before, Python is just one of many programming languages that you are able to choose from. Some are going to be more complex and have more power than you could imagine, and provide more than you will be able to get from Python. The program you will choose depends on the type of work you're doing. With all these other options, why would you consider working with Python over one of the others? Here we will discuss some of the benefits of choosing Python.

Readability

One of the first things you will notice when you get started with Python is that it is really easy to read through. It is based off the English language and the first time you take a look at it, you may give a sigh of relief because it will look easy to read through. Python is also an easy language to learn how to format, as long as you know some of the basic rules. Anyone is going to be able to learn how to write in this language, and it is easy to make something, even as a beginner, that other programmers can read and understand.

Libraries

When you are new to programming, the library of your chosen coding language can be really important. These libraries are going to contain a lot of the commands and syntaxes that you will need and that work inside the Python language. Since this is an open sourced program, there are thousands of codes inside of the library and other programmers are always developing more that can be placed inside.

This is good news for beginners. If you are interested in learning a new code inside the system or you aren't sure where to put something inside the code you are developing, you can head to the library and often find the information that you need. This can be nice when you want to save time. You are able to insert the codes you find through the library into your own code as well.

Community

One of the nice things about working in the Python language is that you will be able to find a good community to work with. Python is one of the most popular coding languages and, because of this, it has a large community. You will be able to find national conferences that will contain many of the Python products and you can easily find forums online where people are constantly asking questions and getting advice.

As a beginner, it is a good idea to check out some of these communities. They are full of more advanced users, as well as other beginners looking for advice, and if you get stuck on something, want to learn something new, or have issues with the programming, this is the place where you will find your answers.

Usability

When you are beginning with a new programming language, especially if you don't have any experience within the coding field, you want to make sure that the program you are using is practical. You don't want to spend months trying to learn how to use new code. There is a little work to learning a new programming language, but most people want to feel that it is something they can do with a bit of work, rather than something that they will never be able to figure out.

With the Python language, you are going to find that it doesn't have a lot of tricks inside of it, and you will find that you can read some of the code before learning anything about it. After a bit of practice, you will find that you can write your own code in no time.

CHAPTER 2

Working With Your Files In Python

There are going to be times when you're creating something in Python, and you will want to store the data in a way that is easy to access at a later time. You may want to have it displayed in the program, as a part or a whole, and you want this to be a simple process.

When you want to store data, you should make a new "file," but you will have times when you can reuse the same code over again inside your program. Let's take some time in this chapter to create some of these files, so that they will stick around when you are creating a new program in Python.

There are a few types of operations that you are able to use and will have carried out when you are working inside of your code and in the file mode. You can think of this like the same process as when you are working in Word on a Windows computer. You will need to save the document inside of Word when you are done when you want to open it back up at a later time. Rather than saving a document in Python, you are going to save the code that you write instead. Some of the operations that you are able to do with your files inside of Python include:

- Create a new file
- Close a file
- Move a file
- Edit a file, to add / subtract code to it

All of these will provide you with choices when it comes to working inside your files and when making sure that the code is where you would like it to be. Learning how to make these work can make it easier to work in Python. After you do them a few times, you will find that the process comes quickly and naturally.

Create your new files

The first thing that we are going to take a look at is how to create a new file. If you would like to write on a file before you get it created, you need to simply open up the file and choose which of the modes you would like to write your code in. There are three basic choices that you can use when opening the file, and these are going to help you choose exactly what you are doing inside of the program. The three configurations used for this include mode(x), append(a), or write(w). Any time that you want to make changes to the file, such as writing inside of it, you will want to use the write(w) mode to get this started.

If we are working on creating a new file by writing out statements or strings (which is what will happen with most of our binary files), you will need to stick with the write(w) method. You will be able to write out the code that you want to use while creating a new file.

You can get a new file started by writing your code, or you can make changes to what is already inside the file. It depends on what you would like to see inside of your code when you are done. The following is an example of how to use the write(w) function to get a new file started inside of Python:

#file handling operations
#writing to a new file hello.txt
f = open('hello.txt', 'w', encoding = 'utf-8')
f.write("Hello Python Developers!")
f.write("Welcome to Python World")
f.flush()
f.close()

When you are working on this particular code, you are telling the compiler that you want everything created in this file to end up in the current directory, since you didn't instruct the system to send everything to a different location. If you would like to find this file, you would look for the hello.txt file inside your current directory. Take a moment to look for this file and then try to get it to open. You should notice that there will be a message that comes up on your screen that says, "Hello Python Developers! Welcome to Python World!" This will that mean you typed everything into the code properly.

Now that we have written a bit of simple code, it is time to take it to the next step. You could choose to rewrite some of the parts of this file so that it will show up with different messages on the screen. You will need to make changes to the code that you are using, but this is still a simple process to complete. Below is an example of what to do when you want to make changes to your syntax in order to rewrite your code:

```
#file handling operations
#writing to a new file hello.txt
f = open('hello.txt', 'w', encoding = 'utf-8')
f.write("Hello Python Developers!")
f.write("Welcome to Python World")
mylist = ["Apple", "Orange", "Banana"]
#writelines() is used to write multiple lines in to the file
f.write(mylist)
f.flush()
f.close()
```

You will be able to write in as many of these lines as you would like to get good results. If you typed all of this inside of your compiler and asked the compiler to interpret the results, you would get this message to come across your screen: "Hello Python Developers! Welcome to Python World. Apple Orange Banana."

Working on your binary files

In some instances, when you are working on your data, you may want to write it as a binary file. You will simply be writing out your data as a sound or image file rather than a text file. You can easily change any of the text that you are working on into a binary file, regardless of the file type that you were using in the beginning. You just need to follow the right steps to get it changed. You must remember to supply the data into the object form, so that the compiler is able to expose this as a byte. A good way to write out the syntax for doing this includes:

 # write binary data to a file
 # writing the file hello.dat write binary mode
F = open('hello.dat', 'wb')
 # writing as byte strings
f.write(b"I am writing data in binary file!/n")
f.write(b"Let's write another list/n")
f.close()

Once this has been written into the compiler, you can then bring up Notepad so that you can see what has been written for the program. It is important to remember that you must decode and encode your functions so that it is easier to read and write with these codes once you are in the binary file mode. To get this to happen, you will just need to write out the following syntax:

 # write binary data to a file
 # writing the file hello.dat write binary mode
f = open('hello.dat', 'wb')
text = "Hello World"
f.write(text.encode('utf-8'))
f.close()

Opening up a new file

Now it is time to move over to opening the files that you have saved so that you can use them again. Any code that you have saved this far has been stored inside whichever computer you are using. You just need to find them, bring them back up, and you will be able to read through them. The syntax that you should use when you want to open the file is:

 # read binary data to a file
#writing the file hello.dat write append binary mode

with open("hello.dat", 'rb') as f:

```
    data = f.read()
    text = data.decode('utf-8'(
print(text)
```

The output that you would get from inputting this into the system would be like the following:

Hello world!
This is a demo using with
This file contains three lines
Hello world
This is a demo using with

This file contains three lines.

You can use this to open up any of the files that are on your system. This is a simple syntax, and makes it easier to find the files that you would like and open them so that you can either read them again, make some changes, or use the code that you have written. As you can see, this is a simple process – part of why Python is so popular to use.

Moving your files

In addition to writing out a new file, saving it, or opening up one of the files that you saved, there are also going to be times when you will want to move the file locations. You may want to put them in a new place that is easier to find, or you may have made a new folder that you want to put a few of the files in for easier access. There may be times when things don't match up the way that you would like, such as words that are not spelled correctly in the code, and making moves could make it easier to work within the files of your system.

You can always choose to move the file locations so that they end up in the right spot, or so that they are easy for you to find in the system. You will just need to take some time to go inside and find the file and tell your code where you would like to have it moved. Once your program finds the new location, you can easily go inside, make the changes, and get them all moved. This may sound a bit complicated in the beginning, but you will find that it can be pretty easy once you try it out.

The trick here is to find out where the original file is located before you are able to move it. For the most part, if you didn't specify where the file should go, it is going to be in the current drive until you move it. You can go to the current drive, or wherever you stored the information inside the system, and open up the file using the tricks that we did earlier. Now that you are inside the system, you will be able to make some changes to the code, choose where you would like to move it (such as giving it a new name or specifying where you would like to place it).

Learning how to work within the files on your system is a great way to get some experience within Python. This is a really good way to start learning how to use the system. It shows how to not only save the code that we will be writing in this guidebook, but also to open it up later when you would like to use it again, as well as how to move the code to a new location if needed. Learning how to do some of these simple steps is the right way to get the program written fast.

CHAPTER 3

Expressions Inside The Python Program

While there are a lot of things that can make working inside the Python language more enjoyable, one thing that you will enjoy the most is the library that comes with it. This is going to make it much easier to get the code that you are working on to come out the way that you would like. When working inside of the Python library, you are working with things that are known as regular expressions. These are the parts that are responsible for executing any task that you want without any glitches. They will also help to handle the searches that you perform. There are many times when you will need to use these regular expressions to help filter your text, and you can use them to check on the strings of text to see if they match up with some of the regular expressions you are working on.

Once you learn how to use regular expressions inside of Python, you are going to be set. The syntax that you are working with will stay the same whether you are working in just Python, or if you combine Python with one of the other coding languages. The syntax for those other coding languages is going to be similar to the syntax that you find inside of Python. Once you learn how to do one of the coding languages, it should be much easier to work with some of the others.

One way that you can see regular expressions and how they function is to find a word that you spelled differently inside the text editor. This could be a misspelling or some other issue, but let's say that you spelled the word "blue" one time, and then the next as "bleu". Even though these are going to have different spellings, you will be able to use your text editor to make the two work together correctly.

Now, when you want to take these regular expressions and make them work inside of your program, you must make sure that you are importing the right expressions from the Python library. A good place to do this is right at the beginning of your program to keep things organized. When you open up the program, you can go through the process and import all the expressions that you need out of the library. This not only helps you to write out the code that you should be using, but it is also easier on those who are trying to read your program later on.

There are many expressions that are found inside the Python library and you will need to take a look at them and figure out the one that is right for your needs. Often these expressions are going to be used at the same time as the statements, so that the statements are able to execute in the proper way. This means that you need to have a good understanding of how each expression works. If you use the wrong one with your statements, you could end up with the wrong execution.

Luckily, there are many expressions that you are able to use inside of your code and you will be able to find the one that will help the program work the way that you would like. You simply need to learn how these expressions work and place the right ones in the code, and then you will see that your commands will quickly come to life.

Basic Patterns

In addition to helping you to set up the commands that you want your statements to execute, you will also find that these regular expressions are good at helping you to make up and specify the patterns that you should have within your code. There are a number of different patterns that can be used inside of the Python programming. These include:

1. Ordinary characters. These are characters that will match themselves exactly. Be careful with using some of these because they do have special meanings inside of Python. The characters that you will need to watch out for include [], *, ^, $

2. The period—this is going to match any single except the new line symbol of '\n'

3. 3. \w—this is the lowercase w that is going to match the "word" character. This can be a letter, a digit, or an underscore. Keep in mind that this is the mnemonic, and that it is going to match a single word character rather than the whole word.

4. \b—this is the boundary between a non-word and a word.

5. \s—this is going to match a single white space character including the form, form, tab, return, newline, and even space. If you do \S, you are talking about any character that is not a white space.

6. ^ = start, $ = end—these are going to match to the end or the start of your string.

7. \t, \n, \r—these are going to stand for tab, newline, and return.

8. \d—this is the decimal digit for all numbers between 0 and 9. Some of the older regex utilities will not support this so be careful when using it

9. \ --this is going to inhibit how special the character is. You use this if you are uncertain about whether the character has some special meaning or not, to ensure that it is treated just like another character.

Make sure you learn how these patterns work because they are going to help you to communicate with the interpreter, and let it know what you are working on inside the code you create. You should learn how some of these symbols work and practice inside the interpreter to see what is going to happen when you try out different things. If you use the symbols in the correct way, you will find that your code is going to execute beautifully and there shouldn't be any problems. On the other hand, if you mess up on a sign or on something else within the code, you may find that you get an error message, the interpreter gets a bit confused, or the wrong messages come up on your screen.

Doing a query with the help of expressions

At this point, we are going to work on using expressions in order to create a query. There are a few different queries that you will be able to use, and these often depend on what you want the regular expression to do.. There are three types of methods that work for this kind of action and they include:

re.findall()
re.match()
re.search()

Right now these are all just words in the code that you may not understand all that well, but in the next few parts, we are going to look at what each of them means, how these options are different from each other, and help you to learn when you are supposed to use each one in your code writing.

The search method

Using the search method in your coding is easy. You just need to use the search() as the syntax and you are ready to go. This one is going to be nice. You are able to match together things anywhere, and you won't be restricted to finding matches that are at the beginning of the string like you would with some of the other query options. If you want to look through the whole string and see if there are any matches to what you are looking for inside that string, the search() function is the one that is right for you. To get a good idea of what is going on with this option, check out the following syntax:

```
import re
string = 'apple, orange, mango, orange'
match = re.search(r'orange', string)
print(match.group(0))
```

When you take time to place this code into your interpreter, you will find that the output is going to be "orange". You will be able to find the pattern whether it is at the beginning of the code or later on. You need to remember that with the search() function, it is only going to find the code for you once. In this example the search function found that there was one match of orange because that is all that is there. But, you could have ten more oranges in this code, and it is only going to show the word "orange" once since that is the word that has a match.

Match Method

Now we are going to move on to the second query option that you can work with. This option is going to be slightly different compared to the search function that we did above, but it can also be helpful inside of the Python language. Using the match function is going to find the matches that show up right at the beginning of the string. If there is a match that occurs anywhere except right at the beginning of the string, it is not going to show up in the code.

So when you take a look at the code that we had in the last section, if you used the match function, you would find that nothing would come up in the output. Yes, there is the pattern of using orange throughout the code, but since the word orange is not the first word in the string, the match function is not going to work. And since apple doesn't have a match throughout the rest of the string, you will end up with no results. If apple was recurring, or if you moved the orange around to be the first word in the string, then these could be the outputs to these codes.

This option is going to be helpful if you have a term at the beginning of the string and you want to do a quick look through the statement to see if there are any patterns that match up with the first word. It can save you time when looking for the patterns that you want to use.

The findall method

The next command that we are going to look at when we are in Python is the findall method. If you are working with a statement and you would like to discover all of one word out of this string, using the findall method is going to be one of the best choices. While this sounds complicated, it is going to work like the search function, but instead of just giving you one result, it is going to tell you how many of that pattern are repeating inside the code.

So, taking a look at the code we have been using, you could use the findall method to find all of your oranges. It will recognize that there is a pattern inside of the code, and then it will release all of the items that match this pattern. With the pattern that is above, if you used the findall method, you would get two oranges showing up as the output. You can expand this as much as you would like, depending on how many of these end up inside your code. If there is a pattern of oranges and there ends up being 100 oranges in the pattern, then the findall method would pull up a list that had 100 oranges for you to see.

This can be useful if you have a smaller string and you would like to know how many are inside the pattern. But if the string gets long, you probably don't want to use it because who wants to have a list of 100 or more oranges on their screen? As mentioned above, it all depends on what you would like to get out of this code.

As we've discussed inside this chapter, there are many regular expressions that you will be able to work with. They are going to help you to work inside the library of Python and can be amazing for getting you on the right track when it comes to finding patterns. Depending on what you would like to do within the code, the search, match, and findall methods can really help you to get the information that you want.

CHAPTER 4

Working With Exceptions Inside Of Python

As you get further with the Python programming language, you will notice there are times when exceptions are going to happen. Depending on the type of exception, you could get an error message on the computer. Any time abnormal conditions occur inside of your code, you will need to use these exceptions in order to tell the interpreter how it should react to these conditions. There are also times when the statements and inputs work just fine within your language, but because of the program that you are trying to design, you will need to add in an exception that is just for that program. This chapter will take some time to look at how the Python program is going to work with exceptions, so that the code works the way that you would like.

Any time you are working on your code and you would like to show that a condition that is abnormal occurs inside the code, it is time to use the exceptions. There are a few of these conditions that the code won't allow. For example, if you are writing your code, you may find that you put the wrong statement inside or you didn't spell it correctly. This could create an abnormal condition as your Python interpreter is not able to find what you are trying to do and an error message may come up.

In addition to having abnormal conditions occur within the code, there are times when a programmer will be able to add in their own exceptions. In these cases, the interpreter will look at the input that the user places inside and will see that there is nothing wrong, but because of how the code is written, you want to make the exception show. For example, if you have someone who is using your code who is 17 and you don't want to let people who are under 18 place something into the code, you could make this into an exception. You would tell the code how you want it to behave in this situation, even though this would be something that the program would normally allow.

When you look through the Python program, you can see the library has a few exceptions that are already in place. When you want to add these exceptions to your code, it is helpful to have a few of them inside the library to save you time and to show you how they are going to work. There are different types of exceptions that are inside the Python library, including where the program is going to have issues when you try to divide a number by zero (which is going to show an error message) or when you are trying to read past the end of your file.

The nice thing about exceptions in Python is that even when one of these errors is going on, you can make changes to make it work better. For example, instead of having the computer proclaim that an error is occurring when you try to divide by zero, you could change this to give a message that shares why this is not allowed. Instead of stating that there is an error, you could make a message show up that says something like "you are trying to divide by zero! This is not allowed." This tells the user why they aren't allowed to do something inside of the program, rather than just hoping they can figure out what the error message is all about.

If there are exceptions that you would like to have inside your code that aren't found inside of the Python library, this is an option as well. You will learn how to insert your own so that an error, preferably with a message that you set up, will come on the screen and will let the user know that you aren't allowing that answer.

When you are working on exceptions inside of Python, there are a few options that you will find inside of the library that you should look over and learn how to use. They are going to make exception handling easier, and you will really need to understand and use them properly to get the exceptions to work, whether they are exceptions set by the program or ones that you are creating. Some of the statements that you will use inside of Python for exception handling in your codes includes:

- Finally—this is the action that you will want to use to perform cleanup actions, whether the exceptions occur or not.
- Assert—this condition is going to trigger the exception inside of the code.
- Raise—the raise command is going to trigger an exception manually inside of the code.
- Try/except—this is when you want to try out a block of code and then it is recovered thanks to the exceptions that either you or the Python code raised.

Right now, these may not make much sense for how you are going to use them to handle exceptions, but we are going to take some time to talk about each one and discuss how it will work for your particular needs inside the code.

Raising exceptions

Raising an exception is an easy concept. When you are working in your code and you notice that there is an issue with it, or the program is trying to do something that won't work within the confines of Python, your Python program will raise an exception for this kind of conduct. This is due to the fact that the program will not understand how it is supposed to handle these issues. Sometimes, you will find that the exception is simple, you may have named something the wrong way and you just need to make a change within the code. Or there could be an issue with the user trying to divide something by zero, which isn't allowed within the system. A good example of how this is going to look includes:

x = 10
y = 10
result = x/y #trying to divide by zero
print(result)

The output that you are going to get when you try to get the interpreter to go through this code would be:

>>>
Traceback (most recent call last):

File "D: \Python34\tt.py", line 3, in <module>
result = x/y
ZeroDivisionError: division by zero
>>>

In this example, the Python program is raising the error since you are taking a number and trying to divide it by zero. As we mentioned before, when this error comes up, it is going to look a bit confusing to the user. They may not understand why there is an error coming up. Having a new message show up on the screen is going to make it easier to see what's wrong and will seem friendlier.

Making

These messages are going to come on the screen any time that the user puts in something that may not be allowed inside the system. These can be nicer than having the error come up, and if you create the message the right way, you will find that it can actually help the user. With the message, the user will be able to see the things that they did wrong inside the code, and they can go through and make the changes to get it to work the right way. Here is something that you could write out in the code in order to get a message to come up, rather than just the error from before:

x = 10
y = 0

```
result = 0
try:
        result = x/y
        print(result)
except ZeroDivisionError:
        print("You are trying to divide by zero.")
```

If you look closely at this syntax, you will see that this is going to be pretty similar to what you found in the previous example, but there is one change. The program will still see that you are handling an exception, but you will be able to send out a message to the user letting them know that something is wrong in the code that they are writing. Instead of following the top example and having the error message come up, you will have the message come up that says (in this example) "You are trying to divide by zero." This is going to leave the page cleaner and will give the user a chance to go back on and change the input they are doing.

Making your own exceptions

In the example above, we took a look at how to handle the exceptions that come up if your user is doing something that the Python system doesn't allow. In those examples, we took a look at what happens when the user tries to divide by zero. There are steps that you can take any time that you would like to make an exception in the program, even if it is something that

Python does allow. There are programs that you can create where you may not want to allow a certain answer or so on, and making sure that this is handled as an exception in the program will ensure that it is going to work the way you want.

For example, if you want to make sure that the user isn't allowed to place certain numbers into the system, you would want to make sure that there is an exception added in. If you want to make sure that the user is able to add in two or more guesses for the part they are working on, you could also create an exception for that. The trick here is that the Python program wouldn't see something wrong with what the user is putting into the system, but because of the way that you design your program, there are going to be issues if you allow everything. A good example of this is dealing with ages. There is nothing wrong with the person stating that they are 20, but if you are on a gambling site that only allows people 21 and older to play, you will want to make an exception that says that anyone under the age of 21 is not able to get onto the site.

You are able to set up an exception class as long as it meets with the Python rules and follows the rules of the program that you are trying to create. If there is a certain thing that you don't want to happen inside of the code, such as having certain answers, letters, numbers, and other things picked, you need to add in these as an exception to the program. Here is an example that you can follow that will help you to create some of these exceptions:

```
class CustomException(Exception):
def_init_(self, value):
      self.parameter = value
def_str_(self):
      return repr(self.parameter)


try:
      raise     CustomException("This     is     a
      CustomError!")
except CustomException as ex:
      print("Caught:", ex.parameter)
```

Using this particular syntax is going to help you to get the message, "Caught: This is a CustomError!" It is going to show up whenever the user places in the wrong information, based on the conditions that you set. This is a great way to show that there is a custom exception that is going on inside the program, especially when this is an exception that you set up by yourself.

Keeping this in mind, you are able to make any changes to the wording that you would like to use inside this as well. You aren't stuck with leaving the message that we have listed above. You can use this as a good starting point or choose to change it up so it works for your particular program. If you are keeping people out of the program, and you can't allow anyone under 21 to come into the game, , then you may want to leave a message about that in there.

When you are working with these exceptions, you will find that they are going to be defined as being able to do the same things that most of your classes are able to do, but it is best to keep these as simple as possible when you are the programmer. You want to change a few of the attributes to make sure that the right error is extracted from the exception, but not add more than that, otherwise it can get confusing.

It is possible to create modules inside of your program or your code that will bring up two or more errors at the same time. The best way to do this is to create one class that will be the base for which the definition of the exemptions will be listed out. This is going to help sort the exceptions that you want to work with. You can then go through and create subclasses that will take care of all these different classes.

Doing some cleanup actions

Another of the clauses that you can use is one that is considered the try statement. This is one that is also known as the finally clause, because you are going to use this in order to clean up the actions that are going through your program. These are often called the clean up actions, because once you go through and execute them, they can clean up the code, make sure that it is ready for the next part, and make everything run in a smooth manner.

This is one of the clauses that will be used both on the way in with the code and then again on the way out. You can choose to clean up on the way out whenever the other clauses are still left behind in the statement, return statement, continue, or a break. To see how this is going to work, take a look at this example for clean up actions inside of your Python statements:

```python
def divide(x, y):
        try:
        result = x/y
except ZeroDivisionError:
print("Division by zero!")

else:
        print("result is", result)
finally:
        print("Executing finally clause"

divide(2,0)
```

When you go through and execute this syntax, you will see the results:

```
>>>
Division by zero!
Executing finally clause
>>>
```

This is one of the useful clauses to know how to use. It is great for ensuring that all of the statements will be clean and that when you are done with the code, nothing is going to be left behind. It can be really helpful any time that you are worried about how your program will end or there is some kind of issue between switching from one part of the code to the other. It is often used when you are dealing with exceptions and you need to allow the program to move on, even if the exception has been brought up. You will need to experiment with these kinds of actions as they will make it possible to have smooth transitions between your code and will make it work better than before.

Working with exceptions can be a lot of fun inside of Python. They will add in new stuff that you will be able to do, such as helping to bring up messages instead of error signs when working with the exceptions that are already inside of Python and watching to see which of the exceptions you are going to bring up all on your own to work with the program. You may find that as you go along, there are going to be more and more instances when you want to bring up exceptions and make your program more powerful.

CHAPTER 5

Working With Your Objects And Classes Inside Of Python

First, we need to take a look at what objects are going to be inside of your Python code. Basically, the objects are going to be the physical things that you are going to find inside the language. You would be able to point them out inside of your world when you look around. This is going to make it easier for you to keep the whole code in line. In previous versions of many coding languages, especially some of the older ones, it was harder to work with the coding because things could get mixed up, and if you were a beginner, it would be hard to make sure that things didn't get lost.

But many of the newer programming languages have been changed to become object oriented. These are easier to deal with and can be used in a variety of different ways. Python is one of these object oriented programming languages, and you will be able to look at the objects and determine what they are attached to. So if you have a ball inside of the program or the code, it should match up to the ball that you would find in real life. This helps to keep things in order and even a beginner will be able to recognize how the objects work inside of the code.

With that being said, you will also need to look for some of the attributes that are in your code. The attributes are what is going to determine the object. A good way to think about this is to pick out an object, such as a box. The attributes would be the things that you would use to describe the object. So in this case, this is going to be brown, big, sturdy, square, and so on. These should all make sense to others who would look at the box and want to describe it. For example, you would not want to add in bouncing or flying to the box, because these are not attributes that are usually given to the box.

These classes are also going to help you to organize some of the objects that you are making. If there are a few objects that you are using, you will be able to put them all inside the same class so that you are able to find them later on. You are able to make the class be composed of anything that you would like, but it is often better to make the items inside of the class be similar, so that they make more sense and it keeps the code easy to work with. You may have to think this through a little before you get started, but you should be able to organize the objects that you are using into the right classes to help the interpreter do the work the way that you would like.

This chapter is going to spend some time looking at how you should create your own classes, but before we get into this too much, make sure that you remember these important parts:

- When you are looking into a class, the objects that are found in that one are going to be of the same structure, but they can have some differences as well. For example, you could have a class of vehicles, but this could include vans, trucks, and cars.
- Classes should be considered the design or the blueprint of your objects, and they are going to be in place to tell the interpreter how you want it is to behave and how it should run your programs.

These may seem a little complex when you start, but the classes are going to help to keep everything together for you to use. Whether you are looking to put a lot of objects into the same place, or you would just put one or two of the objects in there, it doesn't really matter. The classes will make it easier for your compiler to keep track of what is going on rather than having all the objects floating around inside the code.

Creating your classes

The main thing that we are going to learn inside this chapter is how to create classes inside of Python. Don't worry, this is actually a pretty simple process and once you are able to get the syntax down, it is going to be easier than ever. When you work with your class statements, you are going to work to make a new definition at the same time. For this, you should place your class name right behind the keyword, and then the superclass is going to be found inside of the parenthesis. You should also make sure that you are following this with a colon; if you forget it isn't that big of a deal, but it is considered a good coding practice inside of this language. A good example of this to in work   includes:

class Vehicle(object):
#constructor
def_init_(self, steering, wheels, clutch, breaks, gears):
self._steering = steering
self._wheels = wheels
self._clutch = clutch
self._breaks =breaks
self._gears = gears
#destructor

```
def_del_(self):
    print("This is destructor....")

#member functions or methods
def Display_Vehicle(self):
    print('Steering:', self._steering)
    print('Wheels:', self._wheels)
    print('Clutch:', self._clutch)
    print('Breaks:', self._breaks)
    print('Gears:', self._gears)
#instantiate a vehicle option
myGenericVehicle = Vehicle('Power Steering', 4,
'Super Clutch', 'Disk Breaks', 5)

myGenericVehicle.Display_Vehicle()
```

The output that you are going to be able to get from putting all of this information into your interpreter includes:

```
('Steering:', 'Power Steering')
('Wheels:', 4)
('Clutch:'. 'Super Clutch')
('Breaks:', 'Disk Breaks')
('Gears:', 5)
```

Special attributes that are available in Python

In addition to being able to design the classes that you would like to use with your Python programming, you also have the ability to work with the special attributes that are inside of Python. These are helpful to know about as they will help you to work on your code, while also making sure the interpreter will already know what you want it to work with.

Let's take a bit of time to look at how the different attributes are going to work within the Python code with the following syntax:

```
class Cat(object):
        itsWeight = 0
        itsAge = 0
        itsName = ""
        defMeow(self):
        print("Meow!")

        defDisplayCat(self):
        print("I am a Cat Object, My name is",
        self.itsName)
        print("My age is", self.itsAge)
        print("My weight is", self.itsWeight)

frisky = Cat()
frisky.itsAge = 10
frisky.itsName = "Frisky"
frisky.DisplayCat()
frisky.Meow()
```

When you are using this as your syntax in the interpreter the result that you will get on the screen is:

('I am a Cat Object, My name is', 'Frisky')
('My age is', 10)
('My weight is', 0)
Meow!

Accessing your class members

With the syntax that is up above, we spent some time defining the object as the cat, and then the attribute that went with it was Frisky, followed by your dot operator in order to access all the members that are in that object. If you would like to get the age to assign the right way to Frisky and the cat, you would need to write out this function like frisky.itsAge=10. You can change out any of the numbers or even the name of the cat as you would like to work with your code.

With this example, there were quite a few variables that you were able to use in order to get the class object of your choice. But as you can see, it may not be the most convenient method for you to get the variables that you would like. There are other methods that are in place that will help you to get the members of the class to come back out. In your code, using the accessor method is going to be a great idea. It will provide the information that you need and trap it inside the syntax. An example of how this would work inside of Python includes:

```
class Cat(object)
        itsAge = None
        itsWeight = None
        itsName = None
        #set accessor function use to assign values to
        the fields or member vars
        def setItsAge(self, itsAge):
        self.itsAge = itsAge

        def setItsWeight(self, itsWeight):
        self.itsWeight = itsWeight

        def setItsName(self, itsName):
        self.itsName =itsName

        #get accessor function use to return the values
        from a field
        def getItsAge(self):
        return self.itsAge
        def getItsWeight(self):
        return self.itsWeight

        def getItsName(self):
        return self.itsName
```

objFrisky = Cat()
objFrisky.setItsAge(5)
objFrisky.setItsWeight(10)
objFrisky.setItsName("Frisky")
print("Cats Name is:", objFrisky.getItsname())
print("Its age is:", objFrisky.getItsAge())
print("Its weight is:", objFrisky.getItsName())

The output that you are going to get from all of this will be the following:

('Cats Name is:', 'Frisky')
(Its age is:', 5)
('Its weight is:', 10)

While the choice above is going to look like it is much longer than the choice that you originally had, this is actually going to be more efficient. You are going to put the accessor method to work, so that the variables that you place inside the code will work properly. This is a good process to work with when you want to use data hiding or data encapsulation. Encapsulation is going to be finished if the variables are protected or private, but keep in mind that since you are inside of Python and this is an open source language, all of the variable members are public by default.

One more thing that you should remember when working inside of Python is that words like private, protected, and public are not relevant when it comes to accessibility of the material to other people. All of the members in this language are going to be considered, by default, public. This means that the attributes that you set will be public.

Property

Now we are going to take some time to talk about the properties of your code. When we talk about properties, we are talking about the part of the code that will get and then set the values. It will work similar to some of your other methods, some of which we have talked about in this guidebook, but the syntax on these will be easier. A property will be assigned in the same manner that you would assign your variable, and this can cause the setter method to execute.

When you are looking at the cat class that we discussed in the above examples, you will have a setter as well as a getter already in place. The setter property has the ability to assign a value to your member variable, while your getter is going to return to you a value from the variables of the member.

Working with the classes and the objects that are inside your code can make a big difference in the things that you are able to do. The objects can be tied to a physical object in the real world, with attributes that are going to be similar to what you would put with the real object. Then you are able to create a class that is able to hold onto a few of the objects that you are creating. These objects inside the class will be similar, but they can also have differences and still fit into the same class. Learning how to classify things in your code in this manner will make it easier than ever to create a code that you would like to work with.

CHAPTER 6

What Are The Decision Control Structures In Python?

Another thing that you are able to accomplish inside of the Python language is teaching the computer to make big decisions for you. There are times when you will set up your conditions and then the user will put in their input. At times these answers are going to be true based on the conditions that you set and other times they will put in s information that is going to be false based on your conditions. You will need to set the program up so that it can decide what it should do based on what you have put into the system and the answer that comes up.

This chapter is going to show you some of the basics that come from teaching the program you are making to do its own decision making. This will add more power to the program and make it easy to work inside of, while having a few different options come up on the screen.

First, let's take a look at the different types of decision control commands that you can make. Some of the most common that are found inside of Python include the switch statements, the if statements, and the if...else statements. There are also variations of these that you can work with that allow for more options inside of the code.

As a beginner, we are going to start out with the most basic of these decision control commands. This is the *if statement* and it is going to work on the basis of true or false. You will set the conditions that are true inside of your code. Then the user is able to put in any information that they would like. If the program determines that their answer is true based on your conditions, your message will show up on the screen or they will be able to proceed through the program. On the other hand, if the input of the user is determined to be false, the system is going to shut down and stop (we will take a look at how you can leave a separate message for when the answer comes out true later on in this chapter).

This is basic and allows the system to put up one message based on whether the input of user is true based on your conditions. A good example of these if statements would include the following syntax:

age = int(input("Enter your age:"))
if (age <=18):
*   print("You are not eligible for voting, try next election!")*
print("Program ends")

So when we take a look at this syntax, there are a few points to watch out for. If your user comes onto the site and puts that their age is 18 or under, they have matched true to the conditions that you have set. The program will see that the input is true and will provide them with the statement: "You are not eligible for voting, try next election!" But something a bit different is going to happen whenever the user places an answer that is above 18 into the program.

When the user puts in an answer, such as 25, into the program, the compiler is going to read that this input is considered false based on the conditions that you have set. Since this is a basic formula for coding, there is nothing set up for when the answer is false. The compiler is not going to put out the statement above, because that only shows up when the conditions are considered true, but when the input is considered false, the compiler has no instructions with the if statement on what to do in this situation. For now, the compiler is just going to leave a blank screen and will not continue on with the program.

As you can see, this is not the most efficient method that you can use with making decisions inside of your program. While it can help you to get the true answers that come from your input, and it is a good place to get started when you are trying to write out some of your first codes, what are you going to do when someone enters an answer that is not considered true based on your conditions? Do you really want someone to come to your code and then get a blank screen? The program may shut down because their age or some other information doesn't line up with your conditions, even if the information is right. Your user may be older than 18, and it will not make sense to close the program because it doesn't meet with your conditions.

Luckily, there are methods that you are able to use that will make sure one message is going to show up when the conditions are met and then another message can show up when the conditions are not met. This ensures that the user is able to see a statement regardless of the answer that they input. These are going to be the if...else statements.

The if...else statement is going to be in charge of making exceptions to the rules to help the program keep running. You can add in a small l part in order to get the program to work well with the if...else statements and to ensure that the right messages are going to show up regardless of what answer they place into the system. A good syntax for working with the if...else statement includes:

age = int(input("Enter your age:"))
if (age <=18):

> *print("You are not eligible for voting, try next election!")*

else

> *print("Congratulations! You are eligible to vote. Check out your local polling station to find out more information!)*

print("Program ends")

Now with this example, there are going to be two options that will come up on your system. If your user inputs that they are 18 or a younger age, the first statement: "You are not eligible for voting, try next election!" will come up on the screen. On the other hand, if your user inputs an age that is above 19, the second message the: "Congratulations! You are eligible to vote. Check out your local polling station to find out more information!" will come up on your screen.

This is a basic version of using the if...else statement. You can add in more than one option if you would want. If you want to make it so that you have three or four different age groups that people are separated out into, you can make this happen as well. You would need to add in another else portion, as well as the information that will tell the program what message or statement should appear.

Once you have had some time to get familiar with the if statements, it is time to move over to the if...else statements. These will add more options to the whole program and will ensure that your program looks put together and is working properly. No one wants to go to a program, put in an answer, and then find out that the screen goes blank. This is something that can happen when you are working with the if statements because they are too simple to handle some of the different variations that happen in coding. Luckily, you are able to use the if...else statement, which is able to fix this process. Even as a beginner you will be able to use it to make a great looking program.

Working with elif statements

In addition to working with the if statement and the if...else statement, you can also create some elif statements. These are nice because they are going to give the user choices. Each of the choices will have a process associated with it and when the user makes a decision, the processes will occur that correspond with the choice. This is one of those options that are popular inside of games. It is possible to add in as many of the elif statements as you would like to the code, you just need to make sure that you have the right syntax in place and that the functions are going to work the best. To see how the elif statements are going to look in their most basic format, take a look at the following:

if expression1:
statement(s)
elif expression2:
statement(s)
elif expression3:
statement(s)
else:
statement(s)

This is the basic syntax that you are able to use when working inside the elif statements, and you will simply be able to place whatever information you would like into it. This allows you to set up the answer that you would like to work with each of the parts. You will be able to make the changes that are needed to the program in order to get many different choices for the user to enjoy and you can choose which conditions need to be met, as well as what responses you would like to come up, based on the answers that the user is providing to you. So let's take a look at how this would look when it is used in a code and has been expanded out a bit more.

```
Print("Let's enjoy a Pizza! Ok, let's go inside
Pizzahut!")
print("Waiter, Please select Pizza of your choice from
the menu")
pizzachoice = int(input("Please enter your choice of
Pizza:"))
if pizzachoice == 1:
        print('I want to enjoy a pizza napoletana')
elif pizzachoice == 2:
        print('I want to enjoy a pizza rustica')
elif pizzachoice == 3:
        print('I want to enjoy a pizza capricciosa')
else:
        print("Sorry, I do not want any of the listed
        pizza's, please bring a Coca Cola for me.")
```

This code is simple for you to get started with, but let's look at what it is going to stand for and figure out how the user would be able to do it. This syntax is listing out a few options that the user is able to go with, and they can pick the one that they like. For example, the user can look at this code and pick out the number 2 in order to tell the system that they wanted the pizza rustica. If they would rather stick with a Coca Cola, rather than having any pizza at all, they would be able to pick that choice as well. You would be able to add in as many of these choices as you would like to go with the elif statements. If you would like to have ten options, that is fine, it would just expand out in the same method as you see in this section.

These statements are a complex part of the Python system, but even a beginner can learn how to work with them. The options that they will enable inside of your code will be amazing. Try out a few of the syntaxes and codes that we have available in this chapter, and get a feel for writing out these statements in the command prompt, as well as learning how to use these statements to write some of your own code.

CONCLUSION

Thank for making it to the end of *Python Programming: Python Programming for Complete Novices*. I hope it was informative and able to provide you with all the tools you need to achieve your goals.

The next step is to get started with writing your own codes within Python. There is so much that you are able to do when you are working inside Python. You will learn to use this language to work on the decision control structures, how to write out the functions, and even how to work with objects and classes. This is a simple language to work with, and while some of the topics that we discuss within this guidebook are going to seem complex and hard to deal with, you will find they are easy to work with for beginners.

Whether you are looking for an easy way to get into the world of coding and you want to learn how to make some of the programs that you have always dreamed about, or you just want to add a new language to your arsenal, take a look through this guidebook.

Finally, if you found this book useful in anyway, a review on Amazon is always appreciated!

www.ingramcontent.com/pod-product-compliance
Lightning Source LLC
Chambersburg PA
CBHW061031050326
40689CB00012B/2770